OH SO FINE

OH SO FINE

JUMBLELIAR

Dr. Paul Joseph

To order additional copies of this book, contact:
Xlibris
1-888-795-4274
www.Xlibris.com
Orders@Xlibris.com
54801

* * *

To my mother Marcia Bennett. Your strength throughout
the years will always provide me that guiding light for
whatever challenges I ever have in life.
Thank you.

* * *

300 Plus Questions You Must Ask Your Partner

Getting to know someone for building a potential long lasting relationship can be difficult. Relationships seem to have taken 180 degrees turn over the course of the years. What were routine conversations patterns have now changed and the way we address our own feelings when communicating with our current or potential future partner may seem to be difficult to reiterate back our feelings in a clear concise manner. Now the feelings that we express to each other are analyzed and the meanings are interpreted in sometimes positive and negative ways to touch stronger and sensitive parts of our emotion. How many times have you argued with your partner in the past about things that the other person did not comprehend? We always fight to have one person understand our emotions on a certain subject when we ourselves don't even understand our own. When something bothers us, we sometimes refuse to tell what the root cause may be and that may have created significant challenges in your current or past relationships and such cycle continues to be harmful and never ending in your relationships. This is the reason why you must identify key relationship questions that are relevant to your interests and have some shared understanding between you and your partners' values and belief so you both can live a wonderful life together through key compromises.

As we grow older, we develop our individual personalities based on various interactions within our environment. So it would be fair to say that everyone on earth is like a snowflake, all having some unique design inside them that makes them special. Unfortunately, that same uniqueness may create challenges within our relationship. When you have disagreements in your relationship, you must fight fairly. Relationship should not be a competition between you and your partner. Just because you did not get your way this time, does not mean your next disagreement you must win. What you and your partner both must understand is there is no "my way" throughout your relationship. When you start focusing on things such as that, it creates a strong pattern of controls over ones own partner and therefore looses the other person interpretation and cause lack of compromise. Instead, focus on "our way" with sincerity. To truly love someone you must give yourself and every part of your mind, body and soul while sharing your emotions with open communication. This was a hard lesson I learned. I used to close up inside because I felt like I could do things on my own since I was "independent." Independent in this book does not mean financially stable but what I call emotional independence. Unfortunately it took me a while to realize to be emotionally independent did not mean a person should

shut their partner out or deal with their emotions on their own. Emotional independence is the balance between two or more individuals that share ideas and beliefs through compromises to reach a mutually beneficial goal with satisfactory results. Being emotionally independent meant that you understood that there are options when communicating various subjects of discussions both positive and negative in your relationship and you truly understand and analyze each option from both sides then taking the appropriate course of compromise that becomes mutually beneficial to you and your partner.

We all have fought "dirty" in confrontations with our partners in the past. We spoke over them, trying to take control of the conversation, running out, throwing things, or doing something that makes the situation worsen. Some folks even go as far as avoidance hoping that the problem would go away. It never does. Avoidance is the worst thing you could ever do as it will build up emotions over time and create even more problems that would take three times as long to resolve. Have you ever thought about what you are saying when you tell someone you love them? Was it infatuation at that moment because someone looks hot, sexy or perhaps extremely wealthy? Many individuals would say that they are in love with their favorite celebrity, but those celebrities have also been in relationships and had broken off the relationship for various reasons. What makes you think that you can be different? Relationships take a lot more than hot looks, sexy body and substantial income to make a person happy. Yes its true those things may help but it is a combination of that and much more. You can see those same concerns on television, in the papers and with close friends. You may have everything in the world, but once you have a partner that touches you in the most intimate way on an emotional level with strong communication, intimacy, and compromise between the two, both your lives and relationship changes for the better.

The secret to being in a relationship that works has many areas that we could focus on, but one key component stands out and that is RESPECT! Ask yourself when you argue with someone, am I giving that person the proper respect as you would want? Regardless if the person is not respecting your position, you should exercise control over yourself. If the two loses respect, then we all know what can happen. Respect goes deeper with cultural and moral interpretations based on family values and disciplines imbedded within you from various social medium. One example is a

Muslim and a Christian might be able to live together, but you can see the difficult involved with each interpretation of household values. Respect is just that. Having or developing shared values between the two is subjected to interpretations that you both must find a common ground. Yes, you both can disagree but agree to disagree as long as your communication does not create hostile confrontation in the future. A good example is if two people like separate basketball or football teams. It's ok to disagree why one team performance is better than the other, but you can still find love and respect when disagreeing. If you both are fighting about what television show to watch, try rotate watching each other's show to find out both interest and why each of you like your choice of shows. You will be surprised what you might find out about yourself in return. My past partner had enjoyed watching the home improvements show which I thought was very unmanly. However, over time I would sit down and watch her shows and soon found myself trying to incorporate some of the improvements I saw on her shows and applied it to our household. The change in thought process became mutually benefiting by her appreciating my company and myself gaining new knowledge.

The next time if you sense a fight or in the heat of a confrontation, slow down, then bring both yourself to a calm. Do sit down and take sometime to reflect on the root of the disagreement after everything has been resolved. You will be surprise at some of the things that comes up that you can use to benefit your arguments in the future. Write your thoughts down and a few days later discuss it as clear as possible to your partner the way you see it. Never speak over each other and always show the other person respect for them to share their views while your partner allows you to do the same so you both can reflect on possible solutions for any concerns. Try not to degrade your partner opinions as if your partner thoughts are of no interests. To belittle your partner does significant emotional damage that will take months or longer to heal. Another thing note mentioning is if you're about to start arguing and you need a "cool off" period, based on what the subject of the conversation may be, cater your time appropriately so there's not too much time taken. If you're arguing about what time your son or daughter should come home from prom, purchasing your first home, going on a vacation, having the in-laws over or a job placement opportunity that may require relocating to list a few examples, it's ok to take a few minutes to calm down and then get back to a calm conversation. What about if you found your partner cheating on you? I believe few hours

is ok to let yourself reflect on the situation before you say or do anything that may make the situation more difficult. Perhaps working closely with a certified family therapist would be mutually beneficial to exercise control over two individuals that may defined themselves as strong headed when it comes to disagreements. I highly recommend for difficult cases such as cheating, drugs, separation of family, domestic abuse, and religious beliefs that hinders your relationship progress, both of you should seek out a licensed therapist to help find strong balance and compromise. Base your needs on your emotional assessment to determine what you can and are willing to handle if there are ever any challenges with trust. Trust is something that only understanding and time may heal and in relationship, time is something we feel like we don't always have.

Our feelings have been hurt, heart broken, trust tossed out the door but we keep trying to find love and that perfect partner while dating and doing it over and over again hoping the next time our relationship choices will be better. We say we hate our past girlfriend, boyfriend, husband, spouse, or that special someone and yet we kept doing the same thing and now you must ask why? Why do we disagree with the things that our partner have done in the past? It is now best that we evaluate ourselves to see if there are logically thoughts being considered and about the other person feelings as well. Love is a powerful word people say too frequently without knowing what it means and hate is a word with severe consequences. When you say those words now, mean them with all your heart and remember another person feelings is involved and not just your own. The key to finding that special person is to ask questions that are relevant and important to you and your partners' future relationship. You must find out about yourself and know your choices that you could or could not tolerate. After all, what's important to you may not be important to the other person. I hope that these questions in this book would allow both you and your partner to find what matters most in order to live a healthy and prosperous life together.

How to use the book

First, the questions in this book are only for you and your partner eyes and should be kept private from public view. I wrote this book with what I believe are the top 300 plus intimate questions that will help your relationship through your journey of getting to know and understand each

other feelings and desires, in-turn making your relationship a long lasting one. The reason the book is called JUMBLELIAR is because the questions in the book are jumbled so you'll know if your partner may be lying or telling you the truth. You should not just go through the entire book in one sitting but each day you and your partner should spend some quite time in an area where you will not be disturbed. Sit down and write each answer out to the questions asked. For each question asked, you and your partner should try to expand on the answers so its not just a "yes" or "no" answer but builds on each other understanding of your personal feelings towards the subject matter. With every successful relationship, understanding your partners and your own personal desires can only be established through key open and honest communication.

Go through the questions with your partner and answer them truthfully. There is no specific right or wrong answers as each individual is different. Sit down and have an open conversation about each question and why they are important to you both. Some of the questions in the book are challenging and may take some time to address while you get to know each other and become comfortable with answering the questions openly and honestly. Some questions you might find difficult to discuss and may say they are irrelevant. However, if such questions create a strong emotional response from you or your partner, then that particular question in itself may be tied towards your belief and emotions on other subjects that are intertwined with the questions and should be answered. Remember, over time, people change and so do you. Therefore the answers you may get to the questions from your partner now may not be the same in a few months or years from now so you want to keep up to date on you and your partner's interest by reviewing theses questions periodically. The most important thing is to have fun with the questions. Enjoy getting to know each other while growing together in a mutually respectful way.

I hope that you find these questions insightful, exciting and fun as many of my family and friends have. I would personally like to wish you and your partner many years of a long lasting and fruitful relationship with strong open communication each day towards both your future goals as one.

You

1. Where were you born?

   _____

2. What was your name given at birth? What is your full name?

   _____

3. What country citizenship do you hold?

   _____

4. If you had to change your name right now, what name would you choose for yourself?

   _____

5. How old are you? What is your date of birth?

   _____

6. What is your real hair color?

   _____

7. What color are your eyes?

   _____

8. Do you have any piercing?

   _____

9. Do you have any tattoos?

   _____

10. How much do you weigh?

    _____

11. Do you workout? How often?

    _____

12. What is your ideal body weight?

_____

13. What was your favorite age?

_____

14. Why was that your favorite age?

_____

15. Is there a memorable moment in your past you will always remember?

_____

16. Do you smoke?

_____

17. What was your favorite cartoon growing up?

_____

18. What is your favorite color?

_____

19. What is your favorite ice-cream?

_____

20. What store(s) do you like to shop at?

_____

21. If someone was to buy you a gift, what would you like for your birthday, Christmas, Anniversary and Valentine's Day?

_____

22. What is your favorite holiday?

_____

23. Do you drink alcohol? How often?

_____
_____

24. What is your favorite food?

_____

_____

25. What was your nickname growing up? Do you have one now?

_____

_____

26. What are some of your favorite books to read?

_____

_____

27. What is your favorite animal?

_____

_____

28. Did you have pets when you were growing up? What were their names?

_____

_____

29. Did you have an imaginary friend when you where young?

_____

_____

30. What were you like when you were a child?

_____

_____

31. Do you believe in ghosts?

_____

_____

32. If you had a super power, what would it be?

_____

_____

33. What was your favorite toy?

_____

_____

34. Did you sleep with any stuffed animal while growing up?

_____

_____

35. What was your favorite subject in high school?

_____

_____

36. If you could change anything in the past in your life, what would it be?

_____

_____

37. What is the wildest thing you've ever done?

_____

_____

38. If you could live anywhere now, where would you live?

_____

_____

39. What is your goal in life?

_____

_____

40. Do you picture your life different than it is now?

_____

_____

41. What is your favorite show on TV now?

_____

_____

42. Who is your favorite musician?

_____

_____

43. Do you prefer soup or salad? What kinds?

_____

_____

44. Where is the most exotic place you have been?

_____

_____

45. What are your favorite sports to watch?

_____

_____

46. Which team is your favorite sports team?

_____

_____

47. Which single store would you choose to max out your credit cards?

_____

_____

48. What do you do most often when you are bored?

_____

49. Name a person you are friends with that lives the furthest away?

_____

50. What was the last movie you have seen at the movie theater?

_____

51. What is the most exciting city you have been to?

_____

52. If you were a crayon, what color would you be?

_____

53. Where do you want to go on your honeymoon?

_____

54. What are your favorite sports and hobbies you play?

_____

55. What scares you the most?

_____

56. Do you play any board games?

_____

57. What type of movies do you like?

_____

58. What is the best day of the year for you?

_____

59. Do you like to dance? What kind of music?

_____

60. Have you ever been in love? Are you now?

_____

61. Do you prefer to hug or to kiss?

_____

_____

62. If you could change one thing about yourself, what would it be?

_____

_____

63. Where would you like to retire?

_____

_____

64. What's the most dangerous thing you have done in life?

_____

_____

65. What was the first car you owned?

_____

_____

66. What's your favorite color?

_____

_____

67. Do you currently have an active passport?

_____

_____

68. What's your favorite flower?

_____

_____

69. What is a personality trait in others that really irritates you?

_____

_____

70. What is the most expensive thing you own?

_____

_____

71. Do you prefer receiving expensive gifts or ones that come from the heart?

_____

_____

72. Who would you consider to be your best friend?

_____

_____

73. If you could live one year of your life all over again without changing a thing, what year would you choose? Why?

_____

74. What is your educational background?

_____

75. What school activities/clubs were you a member of?

_____

76. What were you like in college?

_____

77. What were you like in high school?

_____

78. Did you play any sports?

_____

79. What type of music do you like?

_____

80. Can you cook? What kinds of food?

_____

81. Do you have any criminal history?

_____

82. What's your favorite meal to cook?

_____

83. What do you like to eat?

_____

84. Describe your typical seven days course meal?

_____

85. Is there anything that makes you embarrassed?

_____

_____

86. Have you eaten anything that would be considered weird in our culture?

_____

_____

87. What is your favorite restaurant?

_____

_____

88. Where do you go most often to eat?

_____

_____

89. Name some of the places that you have traveled?

_____

_____

90. Are there any particular places you would like to visit?

_____

_____

91. Have you ever been on a cruise?

_____

_____

92. How would you describe yourself?

_____

_____

93. Have you ever thought about killing yourself?

_____

_____

94. Do you work out?

_____

_____

95. Have you ever thought about killing someone else?

_____

_____

96. Have you ever killed an animal?

_____

_____

97. Do you own any guns or weapons?

_____

98. What are your views on politics?

_____

99. What country would you not visit?

_____

100. Have you ever been diagnose with any illnesses in the past?

_____

101. Any scars on your body?

_____

102. How do you feel about war?

_____

103. What are you really good at?

_____

104. How do you handle stress?

_____

105. Have you had any operation or medical issues?

_____

106. If you were to write a book, what would it be about and what would the title be?

_____

107. Have you ever been on television?

_____

108. How do you feel about people dating the same sex and cross culture dating?

_____

_____

109. Is there anything you wanted to learn but never did?

_____

110. Have you attended college? Major? Degree completion date?

_____

111. Are you apart of any clubs or organizations?

_____

112. Are you allergic to any food or items?

_____

113. Do you believe in time travel?

_____

114. Do you have any phobia?

_____

115. Do you believe in aliens?

_____

116. If you were stuck on an island and you could have someone there, who would you want to have there with you?

_____

117. Have you ever met a movie star?

_____

118. Does your job require you now or in the future any long distant traveling?

_____

119. What are your career goals?

_____

120. Where in the USA have you visited?

_____

121. Are you currently on any medication?

_____

122. What makes you special?

_____

123. Have you ever been arrested? For what?

_____

124. How would your friends describe you?

_____

125. What are your friends like?

_____

126. Have you ever broken any bones in your body?

_____

127. Do you do any volunteer work or have you in the past? Which ones?

_____

128. Have you ever had a pet that was not a cat or dog? What was it?

_____

129. What was the last song you sang when no one else was around?

_____

130. If time travel was possible, and you could go back in time to change or witness one single event in history, where would you go and why?

_____

131. What are some of your favorite shows on television?

_____

132. Would you ever go skydiving?

_____

133. Who or what kind of person do you want to spend your life with?

_____

_____

134. If you see a person walking, what is the first thing you notice about the opposite/same sex?

_____

_____

135. What would you rather be doing in life right now?

_____

_____

136. Have you done any illegal drugs in the past or are you currently doing any?

_____

_____

137. Is there anything in your past that you regret?

_____

_____

138. Tell me something about you that most people don't know?

_____

_____

Relationships

139. At what age did you start dating?

140. How many long-term relationships have you had?

141. Have you ever been in love? How many times?

142. What is the longest relationship you were in?

143. What is love?

144. Are you flirtatious?

145. How do you know when you're in love?

146. Would you consider yourself a romantic person?

147. Describe the most romantic thing you've done for your partner?

148. What roles did play in your past relationship? Dominant vs. compromising.

149. Have you ever been considered a player?

150. How many ex(s) do you have?

_____

151. What adventurous things you would like to do with your partner?

_____

152. Do you prefer to sleep on the right side or the left side of the bed?

_____

153. What is cheating?

_____

154. If you were having difficulties in your relationship, how would you resolve it?

_____

155. Do you consider kissing a friend on the lips who is of the opposite sex cheating?

_____

156. Are you friends with any of your ex(s)?

_____

157. If the person you were dating got larger in weight, what would you do?

_____

158. Is there a low or high weight limit you wouldn't date?

_____

159. How often do you keep in touch with your ex(s)?

_____

160. How long did it take for you to get over your ex partner after you broke up?

_____

161. If you knew that you did something that emotionally hurt your partner, how would you resolve it?

_____

_____

162. If I met your ex(s), what would he/she say about you?

_____

_____

163. Can you name all your ex's?

_____

_____

164. Have you ever cheated on someone?

_____

_____

165. Name some things that you have done to make your partner feel good?

_____

_____

166. Is there any particular race you wouldn't date?

_____

_____

167. If my ex and I went out for coffee, lunch or dinner, how would you feel about that?

_____

_____

168. Is there any insecurity you have about yourself?

_____

_____

169. Have you ever been emotionally hurt in past relationships?

_____

_____

170. Have you ever broken someone else's heart?

_____

_____

171. Have you ever been cheated on?

_____

_____

172. Is there one particular ex that you would want to get be back with?

_____

173. Are there any hard feelings from any of your past relationships?

_____

174. Did you and anyone of your ex use to argue often?

_____

175. What were some of the challenges you had in your past relationships?

_____

176. Do you have any children? If so, how often do you see them?

_____

177. Have you ever been married?

_____

178. Do you want to get married?

_____

179. What attracted you to me?

_____

180. Has anything changed that you have liked about me now verses then?

_____

181. What physical features do you like about your partner?

_____

182. Have you ever had any issues with trust?

_____

183. Do you keep your house clean or just toss things around the house and hope to clean it up later?

184. Do you want to have kids? How many?

185. Have you picked out kids names yet?

186. Could you date someone for 20 years without getting married?

187. Have you ever lived with any of your ex(s)? Any challenges?

188. Would you want to have any pets while living with your partner? If so, what kinds?

189. Are there any cultural values that you must have in a relationship?

190. Describe various household responsibilities you think a man should do versus a woman?

191. What temperature do you prefer the house to be set at during the day and at night?

192. What are the key elements of a successful relationship?

193. If you were to get married, would you want a big or small wedding?

194. Have you ever gotten into a physical fight with your partner in any of your past relationships?

_____

_____

195. Where do you plan on living when you settle down with a family?

_____

_____

196. Anything you disliked in any of your past relationships?

_____

_____

197. Any estrange ex's from your past I need to worry about?

_____

_____

198. How would you keep your relationship interesting?

_____

_____

199. If you and your spouse were together for a long time and broke up, how would you feel if the other re-marries?

_____

_____

200. How did you communicate with your partner in your past relationship?

_____

_____

Family

201. Where does most of your family live?

202. Do you have any brothers and sister?

203. Are you the youngest or oldest?

204. What is your mom and dad ethnicity?

205. Are your parents married, divorced, or separated?

206. Do you have any family members living around the area?

207. How often do you spend time with your family?

208. Are you more like your mom or dad?

209. What is something unique about your mom?

210. Is there anyone in your family you would consider odd?

211. What is something unique about your dad?

212. How does your family celebrate holidays?

213. Did you all have dinner sitting at a table or something else when growing up?

214. Who in your family was the dominant one?

215. What is most memorable moment with your family?

216. Did you get along with everyone in your family?

217. Tell me something you would change about your family?

218. Is there any history of certain illnesses that runs in your family?

219. Did your family have household pets while growing up?

220. How many times have you moved while living with your parents?

221. Any military members in your family?

222. Are there any special occasions your family celebrated?

223. Who did you have arguments with most in your family?

224. What are your parent's occupations?

225. What is a moment you'll always remember while being with your family?

_____

_____

226. Where around the world do you have family?

_____

_____

227. Does your family have a "family reunion" each year?

_____

_____

228. Has anyone past away in your family that was difficult for you to deal with?

_____

_____

Employment and Financial

229. Are you currently employed?

_____

230. What was your first job?

_____

231. How many jobs have you had in the past? What were they?

_____

232. What was your favorite job?

_____

233. What kind of work do you do now?

_____

234. What skills do you have?

_____

235. How many jobs have you held at once?

_____

236. Have you ever owned a business?

_____

237. If you could be President of a country, which one would it be?

_____

238. Have you ever been unwillingly let go from a job?

_____

239. What would be your ultimate job?

_____

240. What is your occupation?

_____

241. Which career field would you never do?

_____

_____

242. What was your college degree in?

_____

_____

243. What is your current living situation?

_____

_____

244. Do you own a vehicle? Are you making payments or is it paid off?

_____

_____

245. Are you a good saver or do you have problems with it?

_____

_____

246. What is your financial situation?

_____

_____

247. Do you have a lot of things on credit? How much do you owe?

_____

_____

248. What is the total amount of all your bills?

_____

_____

249. Are you in the process of obtaining new debt?

_____

_____

250. Who taught you about finance?

_____

_____

251. What do you picture yourself doing when you retire?

_____

_____

252. What role(s) do you see you and your partner playing if you were living together when it comes to finance?

_____

_____

253. How do you feel about prenuptial agreements?

254. Do you have a maid, babysitter or nanny?

255. How much do you set aside on a monthly basis?

256. What bad choice have you made in the past about money?

257. What is your dream car?

258. Describe your dream home? What location?

259. Do you want joint accounts or separate?

260. Have you ever filed for bankruptcy?

261. Do you have any emergency funds set aside?

262. What are your goals if you have a family?

263. Have you had past financial problems?

264. Have you ever been sued?

265. If you won the lotto, how would you handle your funds?

266. Do you balance your checkbook or swing it?

_____

_____

267. What is the most amount of funds you have saved?

_____

_____

268. How many credit cards do you have?

_____

_____

269. What is the lowest and highest income you have made?

_____

_____

270. How do you diversify your funds?

_____

_____

271. Are there any liens against you?

_____

_____

272. Do you owe any back child support/alimony or are currently paying any?

_____

_____

273. Are there any judgments against you?

_____

_____

274. Do you know what your current credit score is?

_____

_____

275. How much funds do you think is appropriate to retire with?

_____

_____

Sex

276. Have you ever had sex?

_____

_____

277. Do you prefer brief or boxers?

_____

_____

278. Is there anything about your body you don't like?

_____

_____

279. Do you prefer thongs or panties?

_____

_____

280. Do you enjoy kissing?

_____

_____

281. How old were you when you first had sex?

_____

_____

282. What was your first experience like?

_____

_____

283. Would you consider yourself experienced?

_____

_____

284. Have you ever had a one night stand?

_____

_____

285. How many partners have you slept with?

_____

_____

286. If someone slept with over 100 people, how would you feel about that?

_____

_____

287. Do you like public display of affection (PDA)?

288. What is the youngest person you've slept with?

289. Are you able to have children?

290. What is the oldest person you have slept with?

291. Does ethnicity matter with you when it comes to sex?

292. How often do you have sex?

293. What do you like about sex?

294. Would you consider yourself a booty person?

295. When was your favorite time being intimate?

296. Is there anything about sex that you don't like?

297. Do you have any medical or emotional concerns about being intimate?

298. What is the strangest sexual encounter you have had?

299. Public places or private?

_____

300. What sexual feature turns you on most about your partner?

_____

301. What are your sensitive spots?

_____

302. Do you own any sex toys?

_____

303. What is your favorite position?

_____

304. Have you ever been intimate with a person of the same sex?

_____

305. Name some of your sexual fantasies?

_____

306. What is the craziest place you have had sex?

_____

307. Do you like oral sex? Giving or receiving?

_____

308. Have you ever been caught having sex? If so, by whom?

_____

309. Do you like soft sex or ruff sex?

_____

310. What is the longest you have ever gone without having sex?

_____

311. Have you tried a threesome, foursome, etc?

_____

312. Is there anything off limits when it comes to sex?

_____

_____

313. Do you masturbate? How often?

_____

_____

314. What is the longest you have gone without having sex?

_____

_____

315. Do you go online to watch porn?

_____

_____

316. How do you feel about the morning after pill?

_____

_____

317. Do you know how to make yourself have an orgasim?

_____

_____

318. Would you watch porn with your partner?

_____

_____

319. Are there any positions you wouldn't try?

_____

_____

320. How often do you get horny?

_____

_____

321. Are you horny now?

_____

_____

322. Have you ever slept with someone while in an aircraft?

_____

_____

323. Have you had any sexual transmitted diseases (STD)?

_____

_____

324. What was your funniest sexual experience?

_____

_____

325. Have you ever video taped you and your partner having sex?

326. Have you ever been tested for STD? When was the last time?

327. Are there any sexual videos or photos of you that might come back and haunt you such as on the internet?

328. What famous person would you want to have sex with?

329. How do you feel about abortion?

330. When was the last time you had sex?

331. Would you have sex on a lunch break with your partner?

332. How do you feel about porn?

333. Have you ever experimented with animals sexually?

334. What is your fetish?

335. What place (s) would you like to have sex that you have not done it before?

336. Describe the difference between having sex and making love?

337. At what age would you start teaching your kids about sex?

_____

_____

338. Do you like quickies or things planned when having sex?

_____

_____

339. Have you ever had sex while at work?

_____

_____

340. Is there are particular time of day you think most about sex?

_____

_____

341. How often do you think you and your partner should be having sex?

_____

_____

342. What turns you on?

_____

_____

Religion

343. Were you baptized?

344. What is your faith?

345. How often do you practice your faith?

346. Where do you go to practice your faith?

347. What book do you follow for your faith?

348. What was your faith growing up?

349. How does your family feel about religion?

350. How do you feel about death?

351. Are there any values you must have in your relationship based on religion?

352. Would you date someone of a different faith than your own?

353. What religion would play a role during you marital ceremony?

354. Who/what inspired you to be the way you are in faith?

_____

_____

355. Have you ever had a near death experience?

_____

_____

356. Should you and your partner have the same faith?

_____

_____

357. Would you date someone with the opposite faith?

_____

_____

358. Do you believe in heaven and hell?

_____

_____

359. How does science affect your perception about religion?

_____

_____

360. Do you believe in reincarnation?

_____

_____

361. Do you meditate?

_____

_____

362. What are you views on other religious beliefs?

_____

_____

363. How would you instill value of religion as apart of a family to include your kids if you had/have any?

_____

_____

364. What are some things that your faith does not allow you to do?

_____

_____

365. Do you provide financial support to any particular religious group?

_____

_____

366. How often do you pray?

_____

367. Are there any religions you strongly disagree with?

_____

368. If you have kids with your partner, would you baptize them?

_____

369. Are there any spiritual things you would want around your household to be decorated with while living with your partner such as paintings, statues, crosses, symbol, angels, etc.?

_____

_____

Congratulations! Now that you have completed the questions in the book, remember any answers to the questions you wrote down may and will most likely change as the months and years go by. Keep informed of what is taking place in your partners life and your own by having an open communication channel between both of you. In turn, your relationship will grow strong and long lasting. Once again I am wishing you a fruitful, long lasting and beautiful relationship.